7 STEPS TO GETTING A PROMOTION

EASY TO READ GUIDE FOR BEGINNERS

BY ANGELICA MONTROSE

FIRST EDITION 2015

INTRODUCTION

Gone are the days when you worked hard and your boss took notice of all your efforts and offered you a promotion. These days competition is fearless.

Doing your job well is important, but it is not enough if you want to get to the next level.

Having the right qualifications required for the job, completing many training courses relevant to your career and having an enthusiastic approach to work is only some of the requirements to getting a promotion. But you probably found out by now that you need more than that.

In this book I will share with you the key skills, attitude and actions you need to have to get promoted.
There are seven key steps you need to follow in order to get a promotion.
In the first Chapter I will help you to understand where you are now and how to get to where you want to be. Planning your career and setting goals is one of the first tools that you need to master in this journey.
In Chapter 2, I discuss the importance of doing your job well, learning new skills and building self-confidence.

In Chapter 3, I will explain why strategic thinking is one of the most relevant skills needed in an organization, what it involves and how you can learn to be a strategic thinker.

In Chapter 4, I will touch on self-management. How having self-management or lack of can affect your environment and future.

In Chapter 5, I will show you how to create the right image and get noticed at work. How others perceive you at work is critical to your future in the organization.

In Chapter 6, I will explain how networking, building relationships and influencing others can lead you to your dream job.

Finally in Chapter 7, I will provide you with the last step to follow and get ready to get your next promotion.

Like Albert Einstein said:

"You have learnt the rules of the game and then you have to play better than anyone else".

DISCLAIMER

TABLE OF CONTENTS

CHAPTER 1

HAVING A PLAN

Are you one of those people who feel that you have been working hard, putting a lot of time and effort and is not getting anywhere in your job?

Do you know where are you heading in your career?

No matter what you want to achieve in life, you always need a plan. You need to understand where you are now and where you want to be.

After all most people do not set out to go on a big journey without knowing where they are going. For some people it might sound adventurous. Not knowing where you are going can take you to only one place, a place of frustration, unrewarding feelings and low self-confidence.

When you take time to think about what you want you come up with strategies on how to get there. You will take advantage of opportunities that you probably missed before.

Before embarking on your journey you must know where you are now.

When you know where you are going, you have a clear path and direction that will take you to your destination. Planning your career is about being mindful of your goals and values and how they match with your work goals. Planning your career includes acquiring and applying new skills and knowledge, seeking opportunities and trying new things.

WHERE ARE YOU NOW

In order to understand where you are now, ask yourself the following questions:

- How did I get here?
- What are my strengths?
- What are my weaknesses?
- What drives me and what is important to me?

Spend time answering these questions. It is not a test; it is pure and simple self-analysis to help you achieve any goal in life and get that promotion that you deserve. Self - knowledge is powerful.

How did I get here?

What were the steps that you took that lead you to where you are today?

Remember that every decision that you have taken is connected to the next decision and eventually brought you here, where you are today.

It is not however, your intentions that took you where you are and neither your expertise or knowledge, but the direction you have decided to follow. So this is the time to think and make decisions. Are you on the right road? Will the next decision take you to where you want to go?

What are your strengths?

Strengths are not talents or skills that can be learnt. They are part of your trait and personality. Strength includes: leadership, self-control, teamwork, fairness, persistence, curiosity, creativity, sense of humor, etc.

Will your strengths help you to get the next promotion? Do you have personal traits that will help you in the next promotion?

What are your weaknesses? Weakness is something that you can improve.

What do you need to learn or improve? Are you too sensitive? Do you lack assertiveness? Are you too demanding? Are you a perfectionist? Do you talk too much?

You might find it useful to do a personal SWOT analysis to identify your strengths and weaknesses. A SWOT analysis is a tool often used in business to develop strategic planning and opportunities, but it can also be used for a product, industry or person. A SWOT analysis evaluates strength, weakness opportunity and threats.

In term of strengths you evaluate what advantages you have over other people in your team. In terms of weaknesses, check what characteristics are disadvantages. Think about the opportunities that are available to you. Can turn your strengths into opportunities? Conversely, what threats can harm you or uncover your weaknesses?

Knowing your strengths to leverage for the next promotion and what weaknesses you can improve and use to your advantage, it will allow you to be better prepared.

What drives you? What keeps you motivated at your work? What is important to you?

Take time to think about what motivates you at works, about your current role, your team members and the place you work.

Some of the tools you can use to help to identify what drives you is the Schein's Career Anchors and Holland's Code test. Schein's Career anchor is a tool that helps you self-assess your career choices based on a combination of competencies, values and motives. The test will help identify what you really want in your career. Holland's code (RAI SEC) is another tool based on 6 personality types and their combination with a 720 possibility pattern. The theory is based on the assumption that people choose their vocation based on their personality.

What drives you is in relationship with what is important to you and your values. Your values are unique to you, their ranking and priority. You recognize your values because they are already articulating themselves in various areas of your life.

When you do things that are in harmony with your values, you generally feel good and happy. When you do things incongruent with your values, everything feels wrong and you can experience unhappiness and stress. Unfortunately we often live under other people's values and expectations.

It is important, but to recognize and understand your own values and respect them when you make decisions and plans.

Think about how you spend your time and energy, feel your space, or spend your money.

If you like reading, you probably have many books in your library or study.

If your family is your highest value, having a job that requires you to work more than 60 hours a week might cause you to feel stress and conflicted.

Determine your values based on what makes you happy and fulfilled. Once you determined your values, prioritize them, by comparing each value against each other.

The good thing about values is that they change with time as your priorities changes throughout your life. What was important to you when you were a teenager might no longer be important now. For this reason it is important to re-evaluate your values from time to time.

Why knowing your values is important?

When you know your values, what is important to you, then you can map in what direction you should be heading. The direction you take should be in harmony or congruent with your values.

When the direction that you take is in harmony with your values, you can feel confident that you are making the right decisions.

By knowing your values, you can now decide if that promotion you are seeking is what you really want or you might realize that perhaps you need to pursue other opportunities.

WHERE DO YOU WANT TO BE

Now that you know where you are, ask yourself where you want to be. You need to be clear on your next position.

Are you heading in the right direction?

Where do you want to be in 1 year from now?

Where do you want to be in 5 years?

Where do you want to be in 10 years?

These questions are basic, but many people struggle to answer them because they are not clear where they are heading.

Do you want to continue doing the same job and get a salary increase or do you want to be promoted to a higher rank or position? Getting promoted to a higher rank or position will attract more responsibilities. You might have to perform additional tasks and learn new skills.

You need to be clear on what are the new demands in the new job, what elements you need to learn or improve.

You can ask your immediate manager to help you draw a development plan to get to the next promotion.

Often, the road to promotion is not straight path. Prepare yourself to be accountable to you own plan. You need to be available to make changes as you go. Always take time to evaluate where you are, where you are heading and how are you going to get there.

To be clear where you are going, you need to set goals that provide you with a long-term vision of what you want to achieve and keep you motivated in the short term.

You need to start with your long term vision, for example where you want to be in 10 years. Sometimes we set goals that could feel overwhelming. Breaking down those goals into smaller goals can make all the difference on achieving your main goal. Write your action plans to achieve your goals. Action plans are task that you need to complete in order to reach your goal. Action plans can be daily tasks that you need to do today towards achieving your long term vision.

One of the most useful tools to help you set goals is using the SMART system. The SMART system refers to defining clear and specific goals that are measurable, realistic or relevant and achievable within a specific time frame. Goals that have no time frames are not goals, just wishes.

If you want your dream job to come true, then set realistic, achievable, measurable task that you can be accountable for and set realistic time frames to achieve them.

When you set goals, write them down and prioritize them. Every time you achieve a goal, reward yourself. Rewarding yourself will help you to build self-confidence. Self-confidence is important to keep you motivated. We will discuss more about self-confidence in the next chapter.

Ensure that you review your goals periodically. Change or modify them based on your priorities and values.

Set goals that are meaningful and challenging. To achieve goals you need to develop self-discipline and be committed. At the same time give yourself enough time to achieve them.

CHAPTER 2

DOING THE BEST JOB, GETTING NEW SKILLS AND HAVING SELF CONFIDENCE

DOING THE BEST JOB

To get promoted you need to be doing your job well now. While we know that doing your job well now is not the only skill you need, it is one of the most essential tools you require to get to the next level. To do your job well entails having the skills and knowledge for that job.

Be present in the job you are doing now, do no waste time thinking on your last task and how well it went. Stay focused on your task at hand. Doing your job well includes doing it efficiently and productively.

Do not make the mistake of committing to a task and then failing to deliver. Make sure that you have enough time to complete a task, and if you cannot commit then ask for more time. You need to be credible while doing your job.

You need to be well aware of your role, you have to be a team player and ensure that your team gets the job done.

You need to be part of your team success and support your peers.

Often you require doing more than just your job, you need to show initiative and innovation. You need to be proactive and take the initiative in helping others. You need to be the person that can solve problems and provide expert advice.

Take pride in your job and do it well. People who are proud of their job are usually driven by an inner enthusiasm that allows them to obtain bigger goals.

See every challenge as an opportunity. When we are challenged we learn new skills. When we learn new skills we can do a better job, and when we can do a better job we have the opportunity to grow even further.

Challenges are an opportunity to test you and rise to the next level. Challenges can be external or internal. External challenges come from other people or situations. Internal challenges come within your own limitations.

GETTING NEW SKILLS

Doing your job well often is not enough; you also need to develop new skills to prepare you for more responsibilities. Consider getting further education or doing some specialized courses that might help you in your next promotion. You can do on-line courses or at night time. Your employer might have the facility to help you with professional development courses.

You can also volunteer for new projects. This can help broaden your skills and meet other people within or outside the organization. Getting involved in your community can also help you towards your next promotion.

Learning new skills will help you be more employable. It will strengthen your current skills and open new opportunities. Learning new skills is a lifetime commitment; you never stop learning, therefore you ought to be seeking learning all the time.

You must first decide what skills you want to learn or strengthen. Then you should prioritize them and plan how to develop them or follow through.

To begin with, you have to strengthen the four foundation skills:

- **Basic skills:**
  Reading; finding information, identifying facts and details, evaluating accuracy of reports.
  Writing; recording information, creating reports/letters, and editing information.
  Mathematics; solve practical problems, ability to make estimations, use tables, graphs or charts, communicate numerical information or data
  Speaking; communicating clearly with the appropriate language and tone of voice.
  Listening; allowing other people to communicate, listening carefully.
- **Thinking skills:**

Creative thinking; associate information or ideas in new ways, brainstorming new ideas,

Problem-solving; identifying problems and possible options, put in place solutions.

Decisions making; collect information identify goals, advantages and disadvantages and making the best choice.

Visualization; use imagination, being able to read drawings blueprints or sketches.

- **People skills:**

Social; being friendly, respectful and assertive.

Negotiation; identifying common ground, listening and understanding other people points of view, arriving to a win-win situation.

Leadership; inspire and influence others, ability to make others to trust you, being able to communicate direction and motivate others, ability to empower individuals.

Teamwork; cooperate with others, share knowledge and information, provide support

Cultural diversity; being able to understand and work with diverse group of people, respect other people rights and cultural believes.

- **Personal qualities:**

Self-esteem; recognize how beliefs affects how a person act and feel, making changes to negative beliefs that you might have, believing in yourself.

Self-management; ability to check and manage your own behavior. Ability to control your emotions.

Responsibility; working hard towards achieving goals, being efficient and productive.

Skills specific to you career should also be strengthened depending on the path you want to take.

SELF-CONFIDENCE

When you are seeking a promotion, you need to feel confident that you can do the job and that you are worthy of the responsibilities. That is why it is so important to strengthen your skills and knowledge. But having those skills might not be enough to feel self-confident.

Self-confidence is reflected in your own behavior, the way you speak and your body language. Self-confidence inspires confidence in others and it is important for your success. Self-confidence can be learnt and built on.

Self-confidence is the ability to trust in one's own decisions. Trusting in our abilities to achieve goals and having self-esteem. Building self-confidence takes time but is achievable.

To build self-confidence you need to take pride in what you have already achieved. You need to be able to set new goals and reward yourself when you have accomplished them. (See Chapter 1). Give yourself credit for everything you try; for taking risks to seek new opportunities to learn. Give yourself credit for practicing positives thoughts and self-talk and evaluating yourself rather than trusting other people's opinions.

To feel confident to obtain your next promotion, focus on your strengths, in the things that make you unique. Being confident is not the same as being arrogant.

CHAPTER 3

HAVING STRATEGIC THINKING

Having strategic thinking is one of the most important skills in any organization.

If you want to obtain a promotion in your organization you need to become a strategic thinker to get ahead in the corporate ladder.

If you are focusing only on your work and projects you are limiting yourself and missing out on opportunities. When you see yourself just as an employee or just working for the company, you employer will see you like that also. You can keep doing your job, doing it really well, getting rewarded for it, but that alone will not get you noticed. It definitely will not allow you to grow in the company.

Your approach to strategic thinking will differ if you work for a non-profit organization or for a profit oriented organization. You need to understand the internal and external factors that affect you and how to take advantage of those factors.

You need to think like the organization you work for and become the organization. You need to understand the organization's values and vision.

But what is strategic thinking?

Strategic thinking is the ability to think conceptually, systematically, analytically and creatively. Is the ability to predict and plan ahead. Strategic thinking is a process that can be learnt.

To develop strategic thinking you need to be able see opportunities and the advantages that lead to success. In other words, you need to be competitive.

Strategic thinking involves:

- Ability to anticipate; be aware of you current environment and emerging conditions that can provide a long term advantage. The ability to anticipate requires knowledge of your organization's current environment, their resources, capabilities, competitors and future vision.

  Gain the support of your managers and ask questions about the broader organizations strategies. The most effective way yet is finding a mentor.

- Ability to define objectives and develop strategic action plans. It requires planning skills, understanding tasks, resources and timelines.

- Ability to be flexible, understanding change and changing opportunities.

- Ability to seek advice from others, learning from the ideas of others and feedback.

- Ability to interpret information. Recognize clues, patterns and opportunities.

- Ability to make decisions; being accountable and making decisions even when the information is incomplete.

- Ability to build trust; understanding other people's agenda and what drives them, ability to listen and gaining their support.

When you are climbing the corporate ladder it is important to understand your organization's environment. It is also important to understand the stakeholders that can influence the success of your organization and your own.

Gathering information about your current organization can be a lengthy task. It is important that you take advantage of all your knowledge and resources in order to succeed.

One of the most basic tools to analyze your environment is preparing a SWOT analysis, as we already done for yourself in chapter one. You can quickly examine the strengths and weaknesses of your organization, as well as the opportunities and threats.

In order to identify the big picture, opportunities and threats can be analyzed by applying the PEST analysis (Political, Economic, Socio-Cultural and Technological changes) in your business environment.

Understanding your environment will ultimately help you to identify opportunities, such as making a process more efficient or creating a new product. You can exploit these opportunities to get noticed at work (more about getting noticed in Chapter 5) and getting closer to achieving your goal of getting a promotion.

You also need to analyze your clients and stakeholders. Understanding what drives them is important for your success. In order to understand your stakeholders, its best that first you list them and group them. You can group them in terms of whether they are internal or external.

Once you have identified your stakeholders, prioritize them. You can rank them in order of how they affect your work, from how much influence they have to how important it is to keep them informed. This will allow you to understand what drives them and what is important to them. You want to create an environment of trust and support for your projects and ultimately the future of your career.

Now that you have all this information, your next step is to evaluate your options and select a strategy. Always weight the advantages and disadvantages of each option and that they fit with your own values and the organization vision and values.

When evaluating your options, also check your evaluating process, do not jump into conclusions. Always check if you are making the right assumption and that you have the right information.

CHAPTER 4

HAVING SELF MANAGEMENT

Self-management is a key component that will help you to get noticed at work and progress in your career. Self-management is the ability of having self-control of your emotions and temper. It is also the ability to self-monitor your own behavior and motivate yourself. Being self-disciplined, accountable, working efficiently and being more productive.

Having self-management skills will allow you to communicate more effectively with others, including co-workers, management, clients and other stakeholders. It will also help you plan your day and make the right decisions.

Self-management requires a set of skills to allow you to be more productive and includes:

- Self-awareness and self-control. Self-awareness is the ability to recognize your own behavior and patterns that might cause lack of self- control. Self-control is important to fit within society but also to achieve goals and avoid emotions or impulses that may lead to a negative outcome. Self-control includes self-discipline to move forward towards your goals. To control your emotions avoid self-sabotaging, think positively and be grateful for what you have achieved. When you are able to control your own emotions, you also develop empathy and awareness for other people's emotions and needs.

Improve your self-confidence, will power and focusing on your task at hand.

- Ability to handle stress. When you are unable to handle stress, you can make wrong decisions. You can reduce productivity and lose self-control. Being stressed can also cause more serious consequences such as health issues. Stress is the perception that demands exceeds the individual's capacity of handling a situation. To manage stress you need to understand first where the stress is originating from. Stress can be caused from lack of time management. It can also be caused by other people, the environment or situation where you have no control. Learning to handle stress is desirable in order to be able to take further responsibilities and manage more challenges as you climb the corporate ladder.

- Ability to solve problems. Problem solving is the ability to be able to analyze situations and facts in order to make decisions. To solve problems you need to first identify the problem. Then you need to identify options, evaluating the options and executing solutions. In order to define the problem you need to make sure that you look at the real issues from various points of view. Identifying and analyzing options requires you weight the importance of each option. Consider quality, time available, financial impact, risk, etc. and what is the best outcome. To implement solutions you require to have a plan, consider timelines and resources.

- Ability to communicate with others. Communicating effectively is important to convey information and ideas, gaining support and minimize barriers. Effective communication skills includes: having the ability to communicate formally and informally, verbally and in writing, as well as the ability to listen. To communicate effectively you need to ensure that your message is clear, concise, correct, logical, factual, timely and polite.

- Ability to manage your time. Time management skills will allow you to be more productive by delivering the anticipated results within the expected timelines. To manage your time effectively you need to be organized and be able to prioritize. Planning is an important tool in time management. You might set goals for the month, weeks and schedule tasks to complete each day. Learn to make a to-do list, manage distractions and avoid procrastination. You also need to be flexible and be able to reschedule tasks and your priorities. When managing your time effectively, you have less stress. You also increase the opportunities of getting noticed and achieving your goals. You increase the opportunities to advance your career.

- Ability to take care of yourself. Keeping fit and healthy is important to be able to cope with stress. It will help you with the responsibilities and challenges that arise from your work. It also allows you to feel more energetic and be more productive. Exercise your body, mind and spirit to keep a balanced life.

CHAPTER 5

CREATING THE RIGHT IMAGE AND GETTING NOTICED

Creating the right image and getting noticed at work is one of the key elements to getting a promotion. You create the right image by how you are perceived.

How others perceive you is critical to your job and the image that you exhibit to others.

Having self-management, doing your job right and being a strategic thinker are key skills that you must develop to help with how you are perceived at work.

But is this enough to get noticed? It is unlikely that by having these qualities alone you will get promoted to higher positions in any organization, government or non-government.

You need to combine your achievements and skills with other qualities to increase your visibility at work. Some of these qualities include:

- Making your first impression count; always dress well. Dress appropriately for your position and professionally. Invest in your appearance and look well groomed.

- Be on time; be punctual to meetings, work and functions. Keep the interest of your organization in mind. Ensure that your superiors and stakeholders are never kept waiting for you. Ensure that you are available during major events or at the most critical times of the year for your organization.

- Be willing to go the extra mile, adding value to other areas of your work and helping others. You do not need to be an attention seeker, but you need to ensure that people know who you are. You need to show your qualities and also be a team player. To be popular it is essential that you develop your people skills. Be helpful to your colleagues, supervisor and management. Develop a relationship not only with your boss, but other people that have the power of decision making within the organization.

- One way to getting noticed is helping others to succeed. When you help others you show self-confidence and leadership. Enjoy a strong relationship with your colleagues at work and with key stakeholders. Be willing to share your knowledge and mentor other people.

- Getting noticed requires that you have a wider view of your environment and seek to not only to do your job, but how to influence others through your organization. How can you better serve others, how can you inspire and empower others in your team and organization. Remember that you can never succeed alone.

- At the same time, seek to learn from others and get some mentoring.

- If you want to get noticed at work, you need to create your own individual image. Find creative ways to get noticed, but be aware not to get noticed for all the wrong reasons. Getting noticed is not about self-promotion. Seek to be part a committee, or groups that might be helpful to know, or put your hand up for any special projects.

- Focus on getting results, influence others and create an impact in your work place. Do not engage in office politics, gossip or have a bad attitude. Dis-engage from any activity that can take away from being noticed and keep focus on creativity and innovation in your workplace.

- It is important that you are honest and be yourself. When you are authentic in your behavior you can deliver your full potential. Do not be afraid about challenging others and getting your ideas through to generate better results.

- Network and create good relationships (see more in next Chapter)

- Take responsibility for your actions and be reliable. Ensure that your boss can count on you. Always finish your work, does it well and productively. Make sure that you meet your deadlines and that you deliver your work consistently. Take credit when is due and give credit to your team when is also due.

- Stay updated in your own industry; read magazines, seek training and be aware of the market trend. Keep an eye on what is going on in your organization without falling into gossiping or politics.

CHAPTER 6

NETWORKING, BUILDING GOOD RELATIONSHIPS AND INFLUENCING OTHERS

NETWORKING

Networking is an invaluable skill. Often, people feel frighten by the thought of the word alone, but networking can lead you to your next promotion or your next dream job.

When you think about networking, think about what you can offer. Be the person that others think when they need something.

Networking is an effective way to acquire new contacts and create new opportunities. Networking is a marketing tool for personal introduction and future recommendation.

Networking is not about just connecting with new people but it is also about building and maintaining relationships. Yet not everybody you meet will be in the same category.

Networking includes people that you might need as contacts, people that are your friends and people that you need to help you to achieve your goals. Some of these relationships might be weak and some might be strong.

When you begin your journey of networking there are some principles and tips that you must know:

- **Have your business card ready,** this is basic, but offering a card is a trade. You should give a card and receive one in return. Make it a habit to write at the back of their card what the other person does.

- **Listen**. Give other people the opportunity to share their story and what they need.

- **Have your "elevator pitch" ready**. Describe yourself in less than 20 seconds. Who are you? What do you do? Where are you based? What is your aim? Be aware of your body language, be positive and firm. End with a question relevant to the situation, ask them what they do or how you can help.

- **Differentiate yourself**. What are you best at? What is different about you? Make sure that what makes you different is highlighted in the "elevator pitch".

- **Build trust and reputation**. Building trust is important to build and grow a business, or to advance in your career. Ensure that you always keep your integrity and be accountable for the actions that you take. Building trust and a good reputation will enable you to build and maintain good working relationships. Be the person that people can relay and depend on.

- **Plan your networking.** It is important to know what you need so you can choose potential groups or people that can help you to achieve your goals. You need to have both business and non-business connections. It is important that you have a diverse network from where you can obtain referrals and opportunities. Choose the most trusted and closest associates very carefully.

- **Keep focused**. You need a certain amount of effort to produce results. You need to keep in contact, participate and get involved in meetings or activities. You should be open always to unplanned opportunities that can arise from time to time.

There are many ways you can network depending on your situation and what is suitable for you and your business or corporation you are in. Many networking opportunities can be found in conferences, exhibitions, seminars, training courses, clubs, forums, website, community events, stakeholders meetings, etc.

Networking can be enjoyable and effective. Always be positive, confident and enthusiastic.

BUILDING GOOD RELATIONSHIPS

Building good relationships is another key element to help you advance your career as well as allowing you to be more engaged and committed to your organization. People that have friends and strong relationships at work feel more satisfied in their jobs. They have more opportunities to be part of key projects, become more creative and innovative.

When you are happy at work, you become more productive, you can focus on opportunities and develop you career.

You need to build and maintain good relationships not only with your co-workers, but also with key stakeholders in your organization, clients and customers.

You also need to build relationships with a diverse group of people. Diversity will bring different experiences and knowledge that you can leverage to your advantage. Good relationships with a diverse group of people will expose you to new ideas and perspectives

The more your give to building and maintaining good relationships, the more you will get back.

The most important factor in building relationships is communication.

A good relationship is defined by certain characteristics:

Trust: without trust you cannot build a relationship. When you trust somebody you can communicate more efficiently, be open and honest.

Respect: value other people opinions and ideas, as they should value yours. Mutual respect will allow you to find better solutions, be more creative and develop knowledge.

Self-management: Making sure that you can be mindful of others, having self-control of your own emotions. (See chapter 4).

In order to build good relationships you need to focus on the following:

- Seek training in developing people skills.

- Understand and identify what relationships you need.

- Make time to build relationships. Devote at least 5-20 minutes a day.

- Keep a positive outlook.

- Respect and appreciate others.

- Be assertive and manage your boundaries.

- Practice listening.

INFLUENCING OTHERS

Influencing others has become a very important skill in any organization. Building relationships and networking are the first steps to be able to influence others at work, gain other people support and cooperation.

But what is influence? Influence is the capacity of effecting a person, thing or course of events. To influence someone it requires negotiating, obtaining support and genuine commitments from others.

Influence requires that you work through perceived obstacles to obtain your desired outcome.

We all have the ability to influence others, as influencing others is a skill that can be learnt. First you need to understand the components of effective influence and the circumstances in which you influence.

The components of effective influencing are: leadership skills, negotiation skills, ability to solve problems, working with others and managing change.

One of the most effective tactics for influencing others is the use of persuasion. You need to understand what works in persuasion, motivates and influence other people to do things.

According to Robert Cialdini, there are six principles of influence:

- People like those who like them: People need to develop a network of personalities who support and respect them in their work. People are more easily influenced by other people that are alike to them. In this case praise is an important element in influencing others.

- People repay in kind: Think about what you can give that is valuable to the other person.

- People follow the lead of similar others: people will follow those who they respect. This is why developing good relationships is so important and gaining respect from others.

- People align with their clear commitments: commitment should be active, public and voluntary.

- People defer experts: people follow authority. Make your expertise evident. Ensure that you provide factual and accurate information.

- People want more of what they can have less of: highlight the unique benefits of what you have to offer.

When you combine one or more of these principles, influencing others is more effective, depending on the circumstances.

But what happens when you have to deal with people that you have no authority over them or do not wish to help you?

One of the most useful tools for this case is using the "Influence Model" created by Cohen-Bradford.

This model will enable you to influence others when the other person is resisting you, or you do not have a relationship with, you do not know the other person well or someone over whom you have no authority.

This model has six steps:

Step 1: Approach the situation as if everyone can help you.

Step 2: Focus on your goals. Approach the situation from the purpose point of view; leave aside your personal motives.

Step 3: Understand the other person's situation. How is the other person judged? Ask yourself, what is their responsibility? What is the culture in their organization? What is expected of them? You can apply empathy in this step to win a potential ally.

Step 4: Identify what is important to you and them. Identify what drives them in their organization. There are often five factors:

> Inspiration related factors: these people are inspired by morality, vision and meaning on what they are doing.

Task related factors: These people relate with getting the job done. In this case you can exchange money, supplies, personnel or information. Be careful not to engage in bribery.

Position related factors: These people are inspired by recognition, visibility and reputation.

Relationship related factors: These are people who wish to belong to a team or have strong relationship with their colleagues. Make these people feel connected to the organization or at a personal level.

Step 5: Analyze the relationship: If you know the person well then it is easy to ask what you need. I do not know the person or you are not in good terms you need to build trust and a good relationship before making the exchange.

Step 6: Making the exchange: Here is when you finally make your offer in return for what you need, the "win-win situation". Make sure that at this step you show gratitude.

CHAPTER 7

APPLYING FOR THE JOB AND GETTING READY FOR THE INTERVIEW

Now that you are armed with all the necessary tools and skills it is time for you to get ready to apply for that position to get you promoted. Gone are the days that a promotion is just granted to those who work hard. These days, especially in large organizations, you need to make an application and go through an interview process.

APPLYING FOR THE JOB

Make sure that you apply for the right position. Remember that you have already analyzed where you want to go. Seek for opportunities that will take you there.

When you apply for a job, you often need to prepare three documents, the latest usually for large government organizations:

- A cover letter

- A resume

- Selection criteria

Cover Letter: The letter should be concise, relevant to the job. You should include:

- what position you are applying for

- a short summary of your qualifications

- Short summary of skills and achievements, what do they want to know

- Why you are the person for the job and your contact details.

Thanks them for the opportunity to apply for the job. It should be no more than an A4 page. Also mention any attachments, such as your resume and selection criteria.

Check for any errors, make sure it is professional and that it is tailored for the job.

Resume: You should include:

- Contact details; Name, address, email and phone number. Do not include gender, marital status or date of birth.

- Career objectives.

- Demonstrated Skills: consider what skills are relevant to the job.

- Achievements; highlight any special achievements. These could include goals, sport or volunteer work.

- Employment History: include all relevant history, including work experience and volunteer work. Employment History should be listed chronologically from present to past. Include position, employment company name, years, brief skills and achievements.

- Education and Training: include any relevant qualification and training courses. Provide detail of the institution, course title and date of completion.

- Referees: You might want to include referees or write on request.

Selection Criteria: For most government agencies you need to complete a "Selection criteria".

Address every selection criteria, each selection criteria should provide evidence of the relevant example. Outline the circumstances, what task you completed, what actions you have taken and what were the results. You should address each selection criteria clearly and to the point. You may address each example in the relevant selection criteria in dot point.

GETTING READY FOR THE INTERVIEW

Preparing for the interview is very important in getting the job. There are few things you can do to get ready:

Research: Try to find out who is interviewing you; find out everything you can about the organization profile and background and the job you are applying for.

Research how to answer the most common questions:

- What are your skills and responsibilities?

- Why are you applying for this job?

- Why should we hire you?

- What are you weaknesses and strengths?

- What major challenges have you faced and how have you handled them?

- How do handle stress and pressure?

- How do you evaluate success?

- What are you passionate about?

- How do you work in teams?

- Also have questions prepared for the interviewers.

Practice: Practice answering interview questions and responses with a friend, family or colleague. Think of actual examples to describe your skills. Think about what the job entails and how your skills and abilities can fit within the job.

Get ready: Ensure that you have planned your trip for the interview. Know exactly where you have to go. Plan to arrive 10 minutes earlier.

Also plan your attire the night before. Make sure that is tidy and appropriate for the job.

Bring a copy of your application and a portfolio or other relevant information that you think you might require.

At the interview: Show courtesy to everyone, including the reception staff. Introduce yourself when you arrive and shake hands with all members of the interview panel. Try to keep as calm as possible and maintain eye contact. Listen carefully at the questions before you answer. If you do not understand a question, ask for clarification before you answer. Be honest and do not guess. Keep things simple and short. Do not use slang or colorful language to answer. Pause to think about the question before you answer. Do not criticize former or current employer or boss. Try to be genuine when you answer the questions at the end of the interview shake hands again and thank the interviewers.

After the interview: Think how it went. Make notes of what happened and think about how you can improve. Ask for feedback from your interviewers. Follow up at the appropriate time. Allow two weeks before sending a short email to the interviewers.

Good luck!

CONCLUSION

Getting a promotion is not about working really hard, but yet you need to do your job well. Getting a promotion requires that you learn and develop certain skills, that you open yourself to opportunities and that you are clear what you want to achieve.

In summary getting a promotion requires that:

- You have a plan, a clear understanding on where you are now and where you want to get.

- That you do your job well, that you learn and develop new skills and self-confidence.

- That you develop a strategic thinking. Think outside the square.

- That you have self-management. Learn to control your emotions and monitor your behavior. Be aware on how you can affect others. Have self-control no matter what the situation is.

- That you improve your perception and visibility. Get noticed at work. Get others to trust you.

- That you build a networks and good relationships with a diverse type of people and people that can help you obtain your goals. Develop the ability to Influence others.

- Be prepared to get your next promotion, apply for that job that you always wanted.

Learning the rules is easy, now is time for you to apply them.

Thank you

Thank you for reading this book.

I hope you enjoyed it!

If you liked this book I would appreciate if you could take a minute and

leave a review with your feedback.

Just go to Amazon.com

Look for **"7 Steps to Getting a Promotion"**

by Angelica Montrose

and

Click on "write a customer review"

Thank you!

www.ingramcontent.com/pod-product-compliance
Lightning Source LLC
Chambersburg PA
CBHW040920180526
45159CB00002BA/541